Contents

Chapter 1: Migration Overview

Chapter 2: Attitudes to Migration

Chapter 3: Refugees & Asylum Seekers

Introduction

Expat or Immigrant? is Volume 429 in the **issues** series. The aim of the series is to offer current, diverse information about important issues in our world, from a UK perspective.

About Expat or Immigrant?

Is there really a difference between and expat and an immigrant, or is it just semantics? Immigration continues to be a contentious topic in the UK, especially in light of recent global events. This book looks at statistics around migration in the UK and our attitudes to different types of migration and migrants, such as refugees and asylum seekers.

Our sources

Titles in the **issues** series are designed to function as educational resource books, providing a balanced overview of a specific subject.

The information in our books is comprised of facts, articles and opinions from many different sources, including:

- Newspaper reports and opinion pieces
- Website factsheets
- Magazine and journal articles
- Statistics and surveys
- Government reports
- Literature from special interest groups.

A note on critical evaluation

Because the information reprinted here is from a number of different sources, readers should bear in mind the origin of the text and whether the source is likely to have a particular bias when presenting information (or when conducting their research). It is hoped that, as you read about the many aspects of the issues explored in this book, you will critically evaluate the information presented.

It is important that you decide whether you are being presented with facts or opinions. Does the writer give a biased or unbiased report? If an opinion is being expressed, do you agree with the writer? Is there potential bias to the 'facts' or statistics behind an article?

Activities

Throughout this book, you will find a selection of assignments and activities designed to help you engage with the articles you have been reading and to explore your own opinions. Some tasks will take longer than others and there is a mixture of design, writing and research-based activities that you can complete alone or in a group.

Further research

At the end of each article we have listed its source and a website that you can visit if you would like to conduct your own research. Please remember to critically evaluate any sources that you consult and consider whether the information you are viewing is accurate and unbiased.

Issues Online

The **issues** series of books is complemented by our online resource, issuesonline.co.uk

On the Issues Online website you will find a wealth of information, covering over 70 topics, to support the PSHE and RSE curriculum.

Why Issues Online?

Researching a topic? Issues Online is the best place to start for...

Librarians

Issues Online is an essential tool for librarians: feel confident you are signposting safe, reliable, user-friendly online resources to students and teaching staff alike. We provide multi-user concurrent access, so no waiting around for another student to finish with a resource. Issues Online also provides FREE downloadable posters for your shelf/wall/table displays.

Teachers

Issues Online is an ideal resource for lesson planning, inspiring lively debate in class and setting lessons and homework tasks.

Our accessible, engaging content helps deepen students' knowledge, promotes critical thinking and develops independent learning skills.

Issues Online saves precious preparation time. We wade through the wealth of material on the internet to filter the best quality, most relevant and up-to-date information you need to start exploring a topic.

Our carefully selected, balanced content presents an overview and insight into each topic from a variety of sources and viewpoints.

Students

Issues Online is designed to support your studies in a broad range of topics, particularly social issues relevant to young people today.

Thousands of articles, statistics and infographs instantly available to help you with research and assignments.

With 24/7 access using the powerful Algolia search system, you can find relevant information quickly, easily and safely anytime from your laptop, tablet or smartphone, in class or at home.

Visit issuesonline.co.uk to find out more!

What's the difference between an expat and an immigrant, anyway?

Why do we prefer to refer to ourselves as 'Expatriates', as opposed to 'Immigrants'?

By Camille Brichard

'What's the difference between an expat and an immigrant?'

It sounds like the opening line for a joke.

And yet, as my country is coming running towards its next presidential election, the question of immigration promises to be a central theme. Every candidate has something to say about it, and the question featured prominently during the preliminary debates.

You would think that with the global pandemic, the immobility over environmental issues, and an economy that is slowing down, there would be more pressing concerns to address. But focusing primarily on immigration is just how it goes in Europe (and outside!) these days... Sigh.

The thing is, I refer to myself as an expatriate, but what I really am is an immigrant.

A legal immigrant, but an immigrant all the same.

I am well aware, there is a difference between legal and illegal immigration. The latter is a complex and politically charged question. But that's not what I want to address in this story.

I am just here to note that we expatriates rarely refer to ourselves as Immigrants. And why is that?

What Semantics has to say about it

I used to believe one referred to people sent by their company for a temporary assignment in a foreign country as 'expatriate.' A person coming to the nation on their own would be an immigrant.

Well, I was wrong,

Because according to the *Collins Dictionary*:

> **Immigrant:** 'A person who has come to live in a country from some other country.'

> **Expatriate**: 'Someone who is living in a country which is not their own.'

So the difference from a Semantic stand? There is no difference.

The subtext

I have the privilege to live in a country that is pretty welcoming to immigration from all over the world.

Until recent history, Ireland had lost many of its people to emigration (people leaving the country to find work, mostly going to the US). So maybe they understand better than anyone else immigration is not a decision one makes lightly just to 'steal one's job.'

Also, the Irish economy is currently booming and needs labor. Which does not hurt: Plenty of jobs to share here.

Even so, most people from other countries I have met here still prefer to refer to themselves as 'Expatriates.'

Let's just admit, the word 'expatriate' mostly has positive connotations.

From the executive sent for a few-year stint abroad with his (usually bored) spouse and kids to the modern 'Digital Nomad' working on his laptop from a Balinese beach, there is a tint of glamour attached to the concept.

However, you could argue that on paper, she did not have the qualifications of a 'good' immigrant:

⦿ For one, when she came to France, Josephine Baker did not speak French: Wrong culture

⦿ 'Proper' French people looked down on her showmanship talents calling her dance 'tribal,' 'savage,' 'African'-like.": Wrong professional skills

⦿ She was discriminated against because of the colour of her skin: Wrong skin colour

⦿ And lastly, she was notoriously bad at managing money, which meant she was almost always broke: No existing fortune to inject into the country's economy.

Today, French politicians are celebrating her remarkable life without acknowledging those incredible contributions were only possible because this woman born in Missouri's slums was able to come in the country in the first place.

While the word 'immigrant' ... well, not so much, right?

When we talk about immigrants nowadays, we might as well use the word 'parasite,' people whose sole purpose for moving their entire lives away from their family and friends is to steal the job of a native. No matter if said job is the wonderful opportunity of cleaning the toilets in your local fast food joint.

In the current discourse, immigration is a nuisance that needs to be contained, not a potential resource. We forget that most of us in America and Europe have at least one recent ancestor who moved for better prospects. Because looking for a better life wherever you can find it, it's human.

Good expats vs. bad immigrants?

Our society differentiates the 'good immigrants' (or expats) with the desirable skills, culture, or wallet from the 'bad immigrants' coming illegally to 'steal' jobs and resources. It's all black and white.

We forget that even the 'good' expats can be not so great: Just ask the Balinese government, desperately trying to fight against the massive arrival of illegal digital nomads coming on a tourist visa and staying illegally in the country with disastrous impacts on the country and the environment.

On the other hand, in France today, we are celebrating the induction of Josephine Baker into our Pantheon.

As a musician, a Resistant, and a civil rights activist, this black American woman (naturalized French later in her life) contributed so much to our culture and society that she will now rest honoured among my country's most revered luminaries.

Tomorrow, the same politicians will go back to making life difficult for the potential Josephine Bakers of the future.

So, what's the difference between an expatriate and an immigrant?

On paper, both populations are made of people coming to live in a foreign country.

The change can be temporary or permanent.

The decision is motivated by internal motivations or external circumstances.

But everyone moves abroad for the same reason: Because they hope for a better life.

The only difference is that an expatriate has 'desirable' skills, skin colour, wallet, or religion.

So what's the difference between an expat and an immigrant?

It sounds like the opening line for a joke, but privilege is the answer, and I am not laughing.

30 November 2021

Write

Write a short paragraph describing what you understand an expat and immigrant to be and the difference between them.

www.medium.com

Migrants in the UK: an overview

How many migrants are there in the UK? Where do migrants live? What countries do migrants to the UK come from? This briefing provides an overview of the UK's foreign-born population.

By Dr Carlos Vargas-Silva and Dr Cinzia Rienzo

Key Points

- In 2021, people born outside the UK made up an estimated 14.4% of the UK's population, or 9.5 million people.

- Compared to the UK born, migrants are more likely to be aged 26 to 64, and less likely to be children or people of retirement age.

- London has the largest number of migrants among all regions of the UK, 3,346,000 – or 37% of the UK's total foreign-born population.

- In the year ending June 2021, India was – once again – the most common country of birth for migrants (896,000) in the UK. It regained the top place from Poland, after a number of Polish-born people left the UK. Poles still represented the biggest non-British nationality (696,000).

- About half of non-EU migrants in the year ending June 2021 said they came to the UK for family reasons, while the most common reason for migration among EU migrants was work.

Understanding the evidence

This briefing defines the migrant population as the foreign-born population in the UK. Where relevant, the briefing also provides figures for foreign citizens residing in the UK, as well as for recent migrants – defined as foreign-born people who have been living in the UK for five years or less.

As of the year ending June 2021, people born outside the UK made up an estimated 14.5% of the UK's population, or 9.6 million people.

The size of the foreign-born population in the UK increased from about 5.3 million in 2004 to over 9.5 million in 2021 (Fig.1). The growth of the foreign-born population appears to have slowed as a result of the Covid-19 pandemic, but currently available estimates suggest that net migration remained positive despite a net outflow of EU citizens (see the Migration Observatory briefing, Net migration to the UK). Although the numbers of EU migrants increased more rapidly than non-EU migrants for most of the 2000s and 2010s, the non-EU foreign born still make up a majority of the foreign-born population. In 2021, an estimated 36% of migrants were born in the EU. The share of foreign-born people in the UK's total population increased from 9% from 2004 to 14% in 2021 (Fig. 2). During the same period, the share of foreign citizens rose from 5% to just under 10%.

Over time, the foreign-born share of the population typically rises more than the non-citizen share, because many

Foreign-born population in the UK by place of birth, 2004-2021

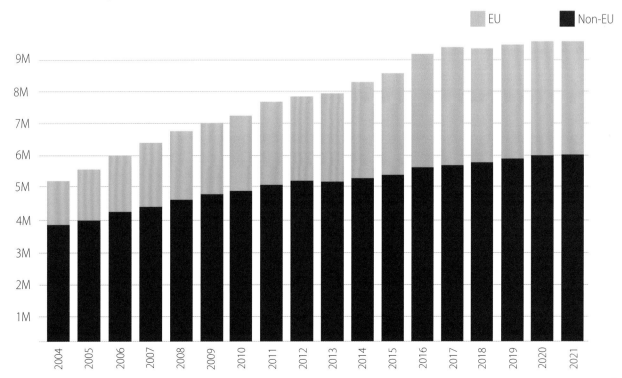

EU   Non-EU

Source: 2004-2020: ONS Population by Country of Birth and Nationality, Table 1.1.; 2021: Migration Observatory analysis of Annual Population Survey 2021

Fig.1

Migrants as a share of the UK population, 2004-2021

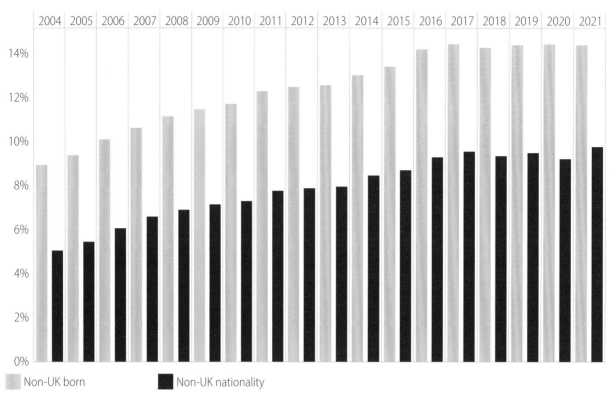

Non-UK born

Non-UK nationality

Source: 2004-2020: ONS Population by Country of Birth and Nationality, Table 1.1. and 1.2.; 2021: Migration Observatory analysis of Annual Population Survey 2021

Fig.2

migrants become UK citizens over time. EU migrants have traditionally been less likely to naturalise as British citizens than people from non-EU countries. This remained the case after the 2016 referendum on EU membership despite an increase in citizenship applications among EU citizens. The non-citizen population also includes some children born in the UK: in 2021, there were an estimated 350,000 UK-born children (under the age of 18) who were EU nationals and 118,000 who were non-EU nationals, according to the Annual Population Survey.

Compared to the UK born, migrants are more likely to be age 26 to 64, and less likely to be children or people of retirement age

Compared to the UK-born population, migrants are more likely to be adults aged 26-64 and less likely to be children or people of retirement age (65+) (Fig.3). In 2021, 70% of the foreign born were aged 26-64, compared to 48% of the UK born. The share of migrants in this age range varies by place of birth, with the highest percentage being for those born in the EU-8, EU2, Oceania, Africa, and Pakistan.

Age distribution of UK's foreign-born population, 2021

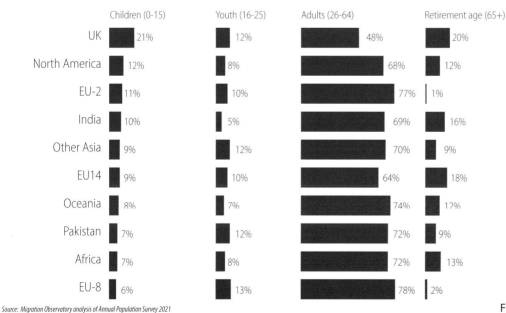

Source: Migration Observatory analysis of Annual Population Survey 2021

Fig.3

An estimated 20% of the UK-born were at least 65 years old in 2021, compared to 12% of migrants. Among the foreign-born, there is a lot of variation depending on the place of origin. Only 1% of people born in Romania or Bulgaria were aged 65+ compared to 18% of those born in the EU-14.

The overall shares of young people aged 16 to 25 are similar for those born in the UK (12%) and abroad (10%). The smallest percentage

Regional distribution of the UK's foreign-born population year ending June 2021

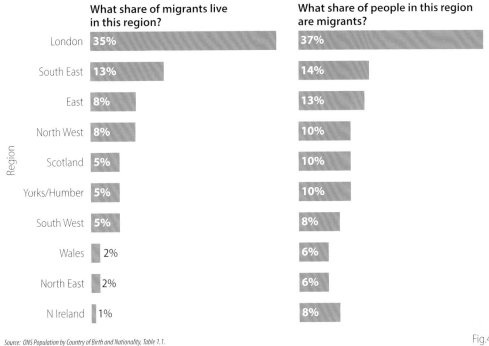

What share of migrants live in this region?

Region	
London	35%
South East	13%
East	8%
North West	8%
Scotland	5%
Yorks/Humber	5%
South West	5%
Wales	2%
North East	2%
N Ireland	1%

What share of people in this region are migrants?

Region	
London	37%
South East	14%
East	13%
North West	10%
Scotland	10%
Yorks/Humber	10%
South West	8%
Wales	6%
North East	6%
N Ireland	8%

Source: ONS Population by Country of Birth and Nationality, Table 1.1.

Fig.4

UK's foreign-born population (48% in total) were either in London (35% – 3,346,000) or the South East (13% – 1,286,000). Northern Ireland, the North East and Wales have a low share of the UK's total foreign-born population, at 1–2% each (Fig.4). In comparison, the UK-born population is more evenly distributed. In mid-2021, only 10% of the UK-born population lived in London.

India became the most common country of origin for migrants in the UK after a number of Poles left the UK

In the year ending June 2021, India, Poland and Pakistan were the top three countries of birth for the foreign-born, accounting respectively for 9%, 7% and 5% of the total (Fig.5). Poland dropped from the first place in 2018, during a period when net migration of people from countries that joined the EU in 2004 was estimated to be negative.

Nonetheless, Poland is still the top country of citizenship of foreign citizens (696,000), accounting for 12% of non-UK citizens living in the UK. This figure is also down since 2018, when it was estimated at 905,000.

(5%) of young people are born in India, and the largest percentage (13%) originate from EU-8 countries.

Although the numbers of both female and male migrants have increased over time, women constitute a small majority of the UK's migrant population. In 2019, about 53% of the foreign-born population were women or girls, according to APS data.

London has the largest number of migrants among all regions of the UK

Migrants are much more likely to live in some parts of the UK than others. In the year ending June 2021, about half of the

Top ten countries of birth and nationality among migrants in the UK

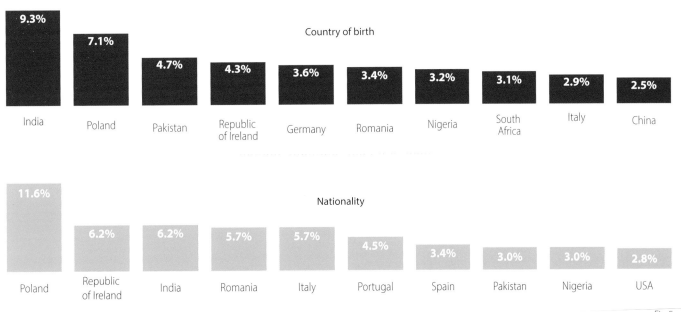

Country of birth

India	Poland	Pakistan	Republic of Ireland	Germany	Romania	Nigeria	South Africa	Italy	China
9.3%	7.1%	4.7%	4.3%	3.6%	3.4%	3.2%	3.1%	2.9%	2.5%

Nationality

Poland	Republic of Ireland	India	Romania	Italy	Portugal	Spain	Pakistan	Nigeria	USA
11.6%	6.2%	6.2%	5.7%	5.7%	4.5%	3.4%	3.0%	3.0%	2.8%

Source: ONS Population by Country of Birth and Nationality, Table 1.3 and 2.3

Fig.5

Main reason for moving to the UK among the foreign-born population year ending June 2021

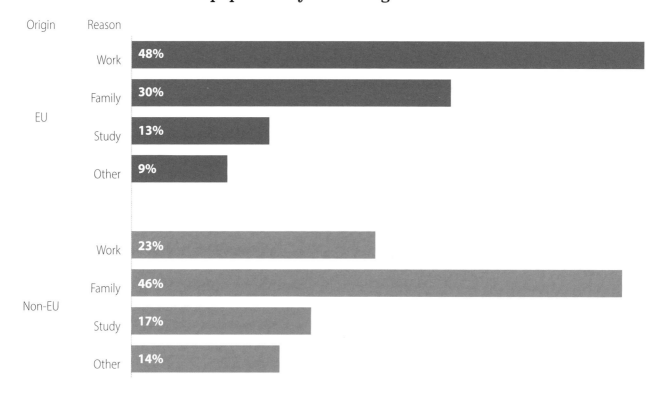

Source: ONS Population by Country of Birth and Nationality, Table 1.5. Note: Excludes residents of communal establishments.

Fig.6

Just under half of non-EU-born migrants in the UK in the year ending June 2021 said they came to the country for family reasons, while the most common reason for migration among EU migrants was work

In the year ending June 2021, the most common reason that non-EU migrants gave for having originally moved to the UK was family (46% of non-EU born), followed by work (23%). The high shares of family migrants in the non-EU population in part reflects the fact that people who come on family visas are more likely to settle permanently than people who come on work or student visas – as explained in the Migration Observatory briefing, Settlement in the UK.

By contrast, EU migrants were more likely to have moved for work (48%). Work was a particularly important reason for migration for migrants from new EU member states, with 55% of EU-8 migrants and 58% of EU-2 migrants giving this reason (Fig.6).

Evidence gaps and limitations

The APS has some limitations for estimating migrants in the UK. First, it does not measure the scale of irregular migration. Second, it does not provide information on asylum seekers. Third, the APS excludes those who do not live in households, such as those in hotels, caravan parks and other communal establishments. The APS is therefore likely to underestimate the UK population of recent migrants in particular. As noted above, there is also increased uncertainty about the estimates since 2020, due to problems collecting accurate data during the Covid-19 pandemic.

There are also some limitations in the APS variable on nationality, which currently does not collect full information on dual citizens. Where a respondent mentions more than one nationality, only the first nationality is recorded. This could mean that the number of non-British citizens is overestimated in this briefing. Respondents' answer to the question 'What is your nationality' will not necessarily always reflect their legal citizenship, and will depend on how individuals understand the meaning of this term.

2 August 2022

With thanks to Veronika Fajth for updating this briefing in 2022.

www.migrationobservatory.ox.ac.uk

Net migration to the UK reaches record high of half a million, ONS estimates show

More EU nationals have left the UK than arrived in the past year, the first negative figure since 1991.

By Holly Bancroft

Net migration to the UK has reached a record high, with 504,000 more people arriving into the UK than departing in the past year, new ONS estimates show.

It is also the first time since 1991 that more EU nationals have left the UK than arrived. Net migration of EU nationals is minus 51,000 for the year up to June 2022, new estimates show.

Total immigration to the UK is at its highest level since ONS started recording the statistics in 1964 – with 1.1 million people arriving in the past year.

Net migration is also at its highest level since records began. The last time net migration to the UK was close to these figures was during the fall-out from the Syrian war in March 2015, when the number was 331,000.

The increase is driven by a rise in the number of non-EU students coming to the UK, and also by hundreds of thousands of refugees from Ukraine, Afghanistan and Hong Kong. The relaxation of Covid restrictions in the UK has also contributed to the 'unprecedented' increase.

In the year up to June 2022, the Office for National Statistics estimated that net migration of non-EU nationals to the UK was 509,000.

Commenting on the statistics, Jay Lindop, ONS' deputy director of the Centre for International Migration, said that a number of world events had driven up migration to the UK in the past year.

She said that international migration patterns in the 12 months to June 2022 were 'unprecedented'.

'These include the end of lockdown restrictions in the UK, the first full period following transition from the EU, the war in Ukraine, the resettlement of Afghans and the new visa route for Hong Kong British Nationals (Overseas), which have all contributed to the record levels of long-term immigration we have seen,' she added.

Migration from non-EU countries, specifically students, was driving the rise, Ms Lindop said. The easing of Covid lockdown restrictions has also contributed to this, as students no longer have to work remotely.

In the year ending June 2022, those arriving on study visas accounted for the largest proportion of long-term immigration for non-EU nationals – at 39 percent.

An estimated 277,000 of these students arrived in the UK over the past year, an increase from 143,000 in the year before.

Study visas and 'Other' visas showed the largest growth in the year ending June 2022

Total number of non-EU nationals who immigrated long term in the UK year ending June 2020 to year ending June 2022

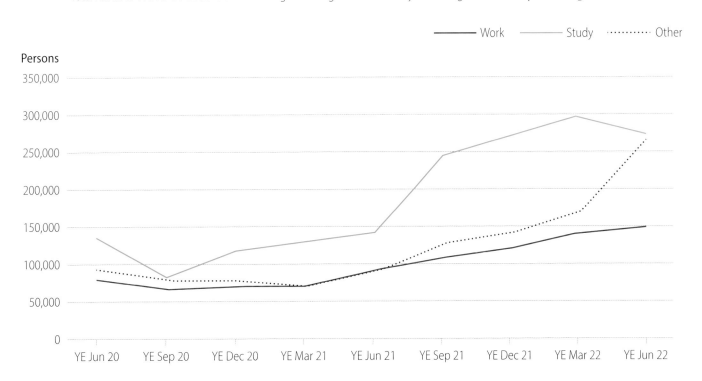

Source: 2004-2020: Office for National Statistics. Publication: Long-term international migration, provisional: year ending June 2022 - Study visas and 'other visas' showed the largest growth in the year leading up to June 2022

Long-term immigration in year ending June 2022 was largely driven by non-EU

Number of non-EU, EU and British nationals immigrating into the UK, between year ending June 2020 and year ending June 2022

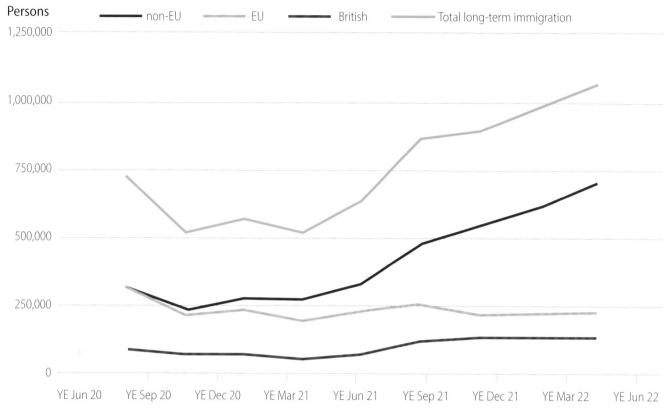

Source: 2004-2020: Office for National Statistics. Publication: Long-term international migration, provisional: year ending June 2022

The numbers also revealed a growing backlog in dealing with asylum claims.

The number of cases awaiting initial decision stand at 117,400, more than twice as many as two years ago, Home Office figures show.

There are now around 80,000 cases which have been awaiting an initial decision for more than six months.

Marley Morris, from the Institute for Public Policy Research think tank, said that the figures told two different stories.

'On the one hand, higher net migration is driven in large part by rising student numbers and the new Ukraine humanitarian routes -reflecting the generosity of the British public in opening their homes,' he said.

'On the other hand, the figures also show an asylum system in serious peril, with the backlog of claims growing further.' Maria Stephens, head of campaigns at charity Refugee Action, said that the 'snowballing delays in processing asylum claims are destroying lives'.

Enver Solomon, CEO of the Refugee Council, said the statistics underlined 'the government's neglect and mismanagement of the asylum system'.

Amnesty International called for a 'complete overhaul' of the asylum and immigration system, saying that the government should provide safe routes for people seeking to come to Britain.

The organisation's refugee and migrant rights director, Steve Valdez-Symonds, said: 'These figures show the UK's system for processing asylum claims remains in complete disarray.'

Over three-quarters, 77 per cent, of asylum applications were granted at the initial decision in the year ending September 2022 – the highest rate in over 30 years.

Home secretary Suella Braverman said in October that she aspired to reduce net migration to the 'tens of thousands'.

Speaking at a Tory party conference fringe meeting, Ms Braverman said: 'In the 90s it was in the tens of thousands under Mrs Thatcher – net migration – and David Cameron famously said tens of thousands, no ifs no buts.

'So that would be my ultimate aspiration but we've got to take it slowly and we've got to go incrementally.

'I think we have got to definitely substantially reduce the number of students, the number of work visas and in particular the number of dependants on those sorts of visas,' she said.

Reacting to the ONS figures on Thursday, Ms Braverman said the record number of people arriving in the UK was 'thanks to the generosity of the British people'.

24 November 2022

France juggles migration hot potato

One correspondent's quest to procure French nationality and the maroon and gold passport that proclaims one a citizen of Europe.

By Alistair Lyon

It requires stamina and determination to become French.

It took me three years to thread my way through a bureaucratic labyrinth from which I emerged late last year clutching a shiny maroon and gold passport that proclaims my citizenship of the European Union as well as France.

I had given no thought to acquiring a new nationality when my wife and I settled in the Pyrenees more than a decade ago, knowing that Britain's EU membership gave me the right to live and work anywhere in the union.

The 2016 referendum that led to Britain's departure from the club punched a sickening hole in my complacency. Suddenly my status was up in the air, just as I was sinking roots and finding contentment in my new home.

A French passport would give me the right to vote and to enjoy travel and other protections within the EU. In the event of the far-right winning power in France, it would also protect me against any harsh anti-immigration measures.

Not that I would be their first target, as a legal migrant and one who is also white, Christian (long-lapsed) and European – like the millions of Ukrainians granted EU protection and the right to work after fleeing the Russian invasion nearly a year ago.

An emotive debate

France is formally blind to distinctions of race, colour and religion. But the politics of fear pervade the debate on migration, especially the illegal kind, focusing on Muslims and Africans escaping war, persecution or dire economic conditions at home.

Far-right populists and nationalists in France and elsewhere talk of an 'invasion' of migrants or peddle theories about a 'grand remplacement' which sees France and Europe as being overrun by Muslim outsiders who threaten their culture.

Such inflammatory discourse, variants of which targeted 20th century waves of migrants to France from Spain, Portugal, Italy and Poland, as well as North Africa, pushes governments towards tough responses and obstructs constructive discussion.

'If you come here and live like us, you are welcome,' said a French farmer I met recently, citing with approval earlier European immigrants who are now well-integrated. 'Not those others, the Muslims, they can't be French.'

He scoffed when I mentioned the millions of people of Muslim origin who are French citizens, many of them born here. For him they don't exist, or shouldn't.

In this view, France is for les Français de souche, understood to mean those who are native-born, white and preferably Catholic, not les Français de papiers (on paper).

Jobs no one else wants

Overall, seven million immigrants were living in France in 2021, or 10.3 percent of the population, of whom 2.5 million have become French nationals since arrival, according to INSEE, the national institute of statistics and economic studies.

Since France does not include questions about religion on census forms, no definitive figure exists for the number of Muslims here. Many immigrants do have Muslim origins, although with widely varying and evolving commitment to the faith.

France has relatively low unemployment at around 7.3 percent of the workforce and manpower is short in many

sectors. But few politicians – or even business people who can't find staff – dare to advocate accepting more immigrants to help fill these gaps.

Asylum-seekers already here are not allowed to work until their applications and appeals have been decided, which can take more than three years in some cases. Most of those who are rejected stay anyway and try to live under the radar.

France hosts hundreds of thousands of immigrants without papers who work clandestinely as care givers, labourers, cleaners, fruit pickers and rubbish collectors and at many other low-paid jobs, unsung and without the rights other employees enjoy.

A new immigration law is in the works. This would make it easier to expel foreigners 'who don't respect the values of the republic and commit offenses,' especially those seen as a security threat. It would also tighten border controls, crack down on people smugglers and make multi-year residence permits conditional on French language skills.

The draft law also proposes the issuance of work permits valid up to four years to attract foreign doctors and other health professionals to a sector under severe strain.

More controversially, the law would allow work permits, initially for one year, to be given to illegal immigrants employed in sectors where recruitment is difficult.

This idea has drawn fire from the rightwing opposition Les Républicains, whose support Macron's minority parliamentary party would probably need to pass the law, and is anathema to the far-right Rassemblement National.

France's dilemma reflects one facing the EU as a whole.

'To mitigate its demographic decline – and to do the jobs most Europeans don't want to do any more – the union needs massive immigration, but many white Europeans do not want to see people of colour and unfamiliar habits in their neighbourhood,' wrote Stefan Lehne, senior fellow at Carnegie Europe.

Jumping the hurdles

Last year I was among 60,109 freshly minted French citizens, including 1,724 Britons, no doubt many of them Brexit orphans like myself.

My quest began in 2019 when I had completed the five-year residency requirement and started compiling my dossier to prove I ticked all the boxes for naturalisation.

I had to produce copious family documents, a lifetime of postal addresses – a challenge for a nomadic former foreign correspondent — plus proof I had no criminal record, had paid my taxes and could support myself.

Once I had distilled my past into a groaning file fattened by translations and copies in triplicate, I had to pass a French-language exam and, last but not least, secure an appointment to submit the dossier and be interviewed by an immigration official.

The crash-prone website for booking them seemed designed to stress-test one's patience, if not one's sanity. It took months before I found a slot.

Before the appointment in July 2021, two gendarmes turned up unannounced at home to confirm my bona fides – and to check me out with the neighbours.

The official who grilled me at the préfecture in Toulouse found light relief in my tangled history from birth in the Congo of Anglo-Scottish parents to cross-cultural marriages and stays in Muslim countries from Yemen to Afghanistan. 'Vous êtes un cas particulier, n'est -ce pas?' I nodded, not really minding being a special case.

She asked me why I wanted to be French. Apart from practicalities, I told her I felt at home here, I had never stayed so long in the same place and had no plans to leave.

She probed my grasp of the values of the republic and laïcité, France's particular blend of laws upholding religious tolerance and a secular public sphere. I had to name five national monuments, rivers, cities, kings, dishes …

My head was reeling by the time the interrogation was over. Now you must wait for a year, she concluded.

I was expecting a letter from the Interior Ministry, but I first learned I was French from our local mayor who discovered my name on the electoral list in June 2022.

A few months later he drove my wife and I to a ceremony for new French citizens, featuring successful applicants from 16 nationalities: Ukrainian, Nigerian, Senegalese, Moroccan, Polish and my German spouse, among them.

Local officials presented us with a welcome pack featuring a letter bearing President Macron's signature. Then primary school kids sang of Liberté, Égalité et Fraternité before everyone belted out La Marseillaise, whose alarmingly blood-soaked words we had learned the night before. To my surprise I felt my eyes misting over.

I will never be a Français de souche. But then an estimated one in four of my diverse new compatriots has at least one foreign-born parent or grand-parent.

My loyalties and identities remain stubbornly mixed up. Who to support when England next plays France in the World Cup? Perhaps Scotland will qualify.

22 January 2023

Alistair Lyon is former Middle East diplomatic correspondent for Reuters. During three decades at the news agency, he covered conflicts as well as political and economic news in the Middle East and beyond. He began in Lebanon and headed bureaus in Jordan, Turkey, Pakistan/Afghanistan and Egypt/Sudan. He spent five years in London as Middle East diplomatic correspondent and five in Beirut as special correspondent, Middle East.

Three questions to consider

1. How do migrants contribute to their host country?

2. Why does their presence lead to controversy?

3. Can migrants be good citizens while keeping links with their own culture or religion?

www.news-decoder.com

Illegal migration bill: can the government ignore the European court of human rights?

An article from The Conversation.

By Kanstantsin Dzehtsiarou, Professor in Human Rights Law, University of Liverpool

The illegal migration bill has been approved by MPs and now moves to the House of Lords. The controversial bill would make it so that anyone who arrives in the UK irregularly (for example, by small boat) can be removed to their country of origin or a third country (for example, Rwanda).

The bill passed the Commons with a number of amendments, including one that allows the government to disregard 'interim measures' issued by the European court of human rights.

The court typically uses interim measures to temporarily suspend an expulsion or extradition of an asylum seeker until their case can be properly heard by the court. These measures are used sparingly, and when the court suspects that sending someone to a particular country could risk violating their right to life, or put them in danger of torture or inhumane treatment. They are not the final say in a particular case – they just ensure that the court has a chance to consider all the evidence before someone is removed.

It is this sort of measure that blocked the first deportation flight to Rwanda from taking off in June 2022.

If the bill becomes law in its current form, the UK would be the only country in Europe that legally gives ministers permission to disregard the legally binding order of the European court of human rights.

According to the court's rule 39, interim measures can be used in cases where the victim is facing an imminent and serious threat to their human rights. For instance, the court can ask a state to transfer a prisoner from a prison hospital to the civil one if they cannot be treated properly in the former. Or, to order a state not to discontinue medical treatment if it might violate a patient's right to life.

The most widespread use of interim measures is in immigration cases. The court can temporarily prevent a migrant from being deported while deciding whether the deportation complies with human rights. If the court finds that the deportation is legal, the interim measures will be lifted and the applicant can be deported.

However, if the court decides that the applicant should not be deported, interim measures ensure that this can actually be carried out – if someone is deported to a country where they face threat of harm, it could be difficult to bring them back.

The court has ruled that failure to comply with interim measures violates a state's obligations under the European convention on human rights (and therefore, international law). The convention, to which the UK is a party, states in Article 34 that parties must ensure the court can effectively deal with applications from alleged victims of human rights violations. Disregarding interim measures would disrupt this.

Complying with the court

Despite regular criticism of the European court of human rights, the UK has a good record of compliance with the court's interim measures and final judgments.

Only once has it been condemned for failure to follow an interim measure. In a 2010 case, two alleged terrorists arrested by UK troops in Iraq were transferred to the Iraqi authorities despite a court-ordered interim measure preventing it. However, in this case, the government argued that there was no objective opportunity for them to comply. The amendments in the illegal migration bill would give power to the minister to disregard international law by setting aside the court's interim measures.

More generally, interim measures are very well complied with. To keep compliance high, the court uses them rarely and only when it is strictly necessary. There are fewer than 50 cases where the court found a state violated the convention by failing to comply with an interim measure.

Russia, which was recently expelled from the Council of Europe, is still the leader in this unfortunate ranking, with around 20 judgments delivered against it. Although Russia has regularly failed to comply with interim measures, this practice isn't part of Russian legislation.

There are some notable instances of compliance with interim measures even in Russia. For instance, when opposition leader Alexei Navalny was poisoned, the European court of human rights ordered Russian authorities to transfer him to Germany for medical treatment, which they did.

Generally, states take interim measures seriously, and even in cases of failure to comply, usually argue in court that they could not enforce them due to some objective reason.

Can they do that?

Put simply, states cannot just disregard valid and ongoing international obligations, such as the UK's obligations under the European convention on human rights.

However, sometimes states do that. The example of Russia again comes to mind, when its parliament ruled that in certain circumstances the Russian Constitutional Court can set aside the judgments of the European court of human rights. This decision was widely criticised by academics, and international human rights organisations.

The European court of human rights is part of an international judicial system that only works if all parties agree and comply. According to the Vienna convention on the law of treaties states cannot use their domestic laws to avoid international treaty obligations. This is exactly what the illegal migration bill now does.

The fact that interim measures are usually complied with shows that they are a respected tool that allows the court to effectively deal with important cases of human rights. They are temporary and can be lifted when a judgment is delivered, but still hold states to binding international obligations. Adopting a legal clause that allows the government to ignore such obligations is a very dangerous precedent that could easily backfire, for example, if the court were to issue interim measures in respect to another member state that the UK government would be in favour of.

To use the football metaphor, imagine a team in the English Premier League suddenly decides not to abide by the offside rule, and introduces this in their team's statute. This would not work in a match, and the team's reputation would suffer so much that it would have much less of a say if, for example, a rival team decided to allow players to use their hands.

27 April 2023

THE CONVERSATION

The above information is reprinted with kind permission from The Conversation.
© 2010-2023, The Conversation Trust (UK) Limited

www.theconversation.com

5 key predictions for the future of talent migration

- **Migrants travel further distances to live in 'cities of choice,' determined by opportunity and quality of life.**

- **While migration is set to increase, what that looks like is likely to change, as predicted by Boston Consulting Group (BCG). For example, more women will migrate, city-to-city migration will ramp up and there will be a fight for residents among cities.**

- **If predictions come to fruition, national public leaders must design a proactive migration strategy to drive economic growth and innovation while building public support.**

Many migrants today travel farther distances, consciously seeking cities of choice – a sociological metric designed by Boston Consulting Group (BCG) that measures and determines opportunity and quality of life. Observed in the aggregate, these migrants are more diverse than ever before and have in-demand vocational skills. They are also becoming more sought-after. While companies have traditionally competed for talent, cities are increasingly competing for residents. Based on the BCG's surveys of 25,000 city residents and 850 executives in 10 countries, we've developed five predictions for how migration will change by 2030.

1. Migration will accelerate

In 2022, there were nearly 40 million refugees from conflict regions. Yet only 280 million people (3.6% of the world's total population) live in a country other than that of their birth. Still, we believe today's trends point to an acceleration of migration. We expect migration to exceed 4% of the global population by 2030, or more than 350 million people.

As large parts of Africa, the Middle East and Central Asia transition to middle-income economies and quality education becomes more accessible, people will emigrate to seek better economic and lifestyle opportunities. Meanwhile, as of summer 2022, the world's largest 30 economies had a record number of job openings,) especially for so-called deskless workers.

2. Diversity is on the rise

In 1990, 45% of migration occurred between neighbouring countries and 23% between countries tied to a common colonial history. Today, only 27% and 17% of migration occur along these lines, respectively. Instead, migrants are more deliberate about their choices and tend to cover greater distances (more than 100 kilometres on average).

Looking ahead, we predict that women will account for most international migrants. Female migrants from the Middle East, Africa and South Asia are increasing, reflecting and driving changes in gender norms that enable women in traditional societies to travel more independently. Migrant women also make a substantial economic contribution, as they are much more likely to work outside the home (64%) than those who do not migrate (around 48%).

3. Migration will become (even) more city-to-city

Cities naturally attract the lion's share of migrants. In large cities, more than 50% of residents will have moved during their lifetime and this number will only increase. Furthermore, more people tend to work in digital or office environments rooted in a common business culture versus a uniquely national one. That leaning is not limited to mega-corporations; many tech startups are hiring globally from day one.

For most migrants, livability trumps almost everything (except salary). A recent BCG survey of digital workers who

and squat on TV studio sofas blame migrants for Britain's housing crisis, for taking jobs from British workers and for failing to integrate. It is at points like this, when the language around immigration gets especially Enoch, that I realise afresh just how many of the public debates on this issue feature neither migrants nor children of migrants. The media, the right often complains, is 'too London'. If that were really true, then 37% of media workers would be migrants, since that is how much they make up of the capital's population. Yet you and I both know that will never happen.

Instead, we get dehumanising language used by both major parties and the press. Immigration is a game of 'whac-a-mole', Westminster sources tell the *Sunday Times* – as if those born abroad should be hit with a hammer. This week, Labour's Keir Starmer complained of uncontrolled immigration'. No doubt he hopes to convey an idea of a government in chaos. But the most direct victims of such language are not the Tory frontbench. New research this week from Hope Not Hate reports a direct link between politicians' use of inflammatory language around immigration and activity by the far right. Braverman hatches a Rwanda plan and the far right share the *Mail*'s front pages. Robert Jenrick bemoans 'Hotel Britain' and the boys in bovver boots lap it up. This all amid a rise in far-right protests outside hotels housing asylum seekers. The violence of such language has a consequence – and it tends to be felt by a mum in a headscarf taking her kids home on the bus, or a grandad making his way out of Friday afternoon prayers.

The narrowness with which immigrants are discussed sits at such odds with the breadth of their experiences.

For her recent book, *The Migrants' Paradox*, LSE professor Suzanne Hall interviewed people from more than 500 migrant-run small businesses, from Bristol to Leicester to Manchester. In long, detailed surveys that took five years to collect, she found a richness and resilience that goes nearly unmentioned. On Rye Lane in Peckham, south London, 61% of migrant business people spoke two or three languages; 28% spoke four or more. In Birmingham, she found a street of shops run by people from Cameroon to Kurdistan to Vietnam. These are communities working in deprived areas, often on the frontline of street racism and in the face of council incomprehension. Yet they plug on, despite 'long working hours, falling wages and rising rents'. The reward for many is not prosperity but precariousness, not citizenship but what Hall calls 'denizenship'. They are both the heart of the local high street and confined to the very periphery of national politics.

You don't hear them whining. Indeed, you may not hear them at all. They've been drowned out by the men who got everything on their shopping list and now have a bad case of buyer's remorse.

25 May 2023

Research

In small groups, create a questionnaire to find out opinions on immigration. Consider the difference between EU and non-EU migrants.

UK attitudes to immigration among most positive internationally

Public opinion has shifted a huge amount in a relatively short space of time.

The UK public have among the most positive attitudes to immigration, according to a new study that ranks the country at the top of an international league table as the most accepting of new arrivals.

Of 17 countries, the UK is least likely to say the government should place strict limits on the number of foreigners who can come to the country or prohibit people from coming altogether. 31% of the UK public hold this view, compared with 35% of people in Germany and 39% in Canada – the next-most accepting countries on this measure.

At the same time, 68% of the UK public think we should either let anyone come to who wants to or let them come as long as there are jobs available – the highest of any nation.

The study was carried out by the Policy Institute at King's College London for a major new research programme as part of the World Values Survey, one of the largest and most widely used academic social surveys in the world which has been running since 1981.

The new UK data was collected in 2022, with the most recent data for other nations collected at various points throughout the latest wave of the WVS, which spanned 2017 to 2022.

The findings underline just how far British attitudes to immigration have shifted in a relatively short space of time:

- In 2009, 65% of Britons thought that when jobs are scarce, employers should give priority to people of this country over immigrants – but this has since more than halved, to 29% in 2022.

- Today only Germany (27%) and Sweden (11%) are less likely than the UK to hold this view. Yet in 2009, the UK was more likely than 11 other nations to think the native-born population should be prioritised over immigrants when jobs are scarce

The UK's increasing openness to immigration is clearly driven in part by positive perceptions of the impact that immigrants have on the country. Of around 20 nations, the UK ranks as having either the most, or among the most, favourable views on a range of impacts:

How about people from other countries coming here to work. Which of the following do you think the government should do?

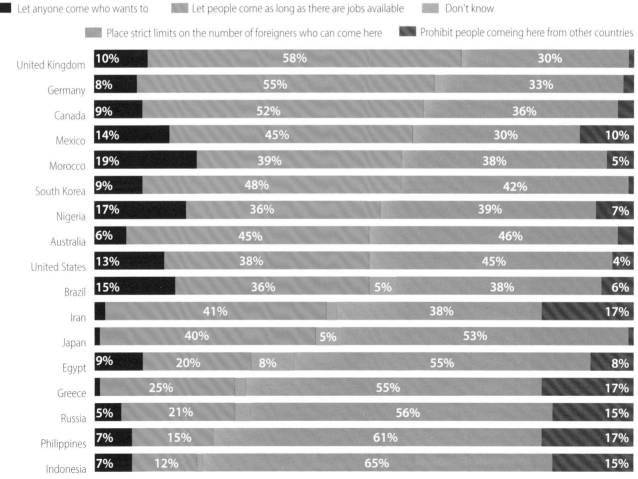

UK base: 3,056 people aged 18+, surveyed 1 Mar - 9 Sept 2022. Other countries all surveyed in wave 7 of WVS at various points between 2017 and 2022, see WVSA website for sample information of other countries.
Source: Kings's College London

- The UK (21%) is least likely to think immigration increases unemployment – far behind countries including Germany (36%) and Australia (36%) and the US (33%).

- Only South Korea (67%) is more likely than the UK (63%) to agree that immigrants fill important job vacancies.

- The UK (70%) is second only to Canada (73%) in believing that immigration strengthens cultural diversity.

- The UK (22%) is least likely to say that immigration causes the crime rate to rise, with countries such as Germany (61%) and Australia (35%) far more likely to hold this view. The UK is also among the least likely to think immigration increases the risks of terrorism (28%).

- The UK (55%) ranks fourth for the belief that immigrants have a very or quite good impact on the development of the country – ahead of other western nations such as Norway (49%), Spain (47%), the US (40%) and Sweden (39%).

However, the UK (39%) does rank more mid-table for the belief that immigration leads to social conflict – on a par with the US (41%) and ahead of Canada (33%), but far below Germany (82%), which is most likely to feel this way.

We've also become increasingly comfortable with immigration on a more personal level:

- One in 20 (5%) Britons said they would not like to have immigrants or foreign workers as neighbours in 2022 – compared with one in seven (14%) in 2009.

- The UK is now among the most accepting countries on this measure – in contrast to similar western nations such as Italy (18%), Spain (13%), France (10%) and Australia (9%), which are all more likely to have a problem with their neighbours being immigrants.

And more generally, the research finds that growing positivity about immigration isn't solely driven by more liberal attitudes among younger people. Views among older generations have also changed hugely – for instance, in 2009, 73% of the pre-war generation born before 1945 agreed that employers should prioritise jobs for people born in this country over immigrants, but by 2022 this had fallen to 38%.

Professor Bobby Duffy, director of the Policy Institute at King's College London, said:

'It was unthinkable a decade ago that the UK would top any international league table for positive views of immigration. But that's where we are now, with the UK the least likely from a wide range of countries to say we should place strict limits on immigration or prohibit it entirely.'

From your point of view, what have been the effects of immigration on the development of (your country)?

Please tell me whether you agree or disagree with the statement: Immigration increases unemployment

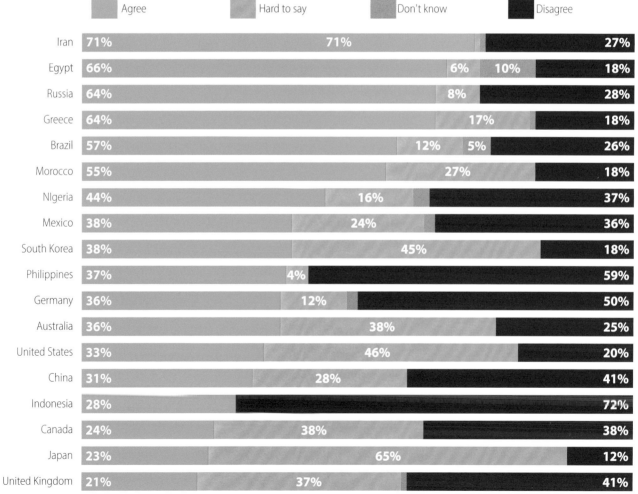

UK base: 3,056 people aged 18+, surveyed 1 Mar - 9 Sept 2022. Other countries all surveyed in wave 7 of WVS at various points between 2017 and 2022, see WVSA website for sample information of other countries.
Source: King's College London

On this list are various groups of people. Please select any that you would not like to have as neighbours. Immigrants/foreign workers (% who mentioned group)

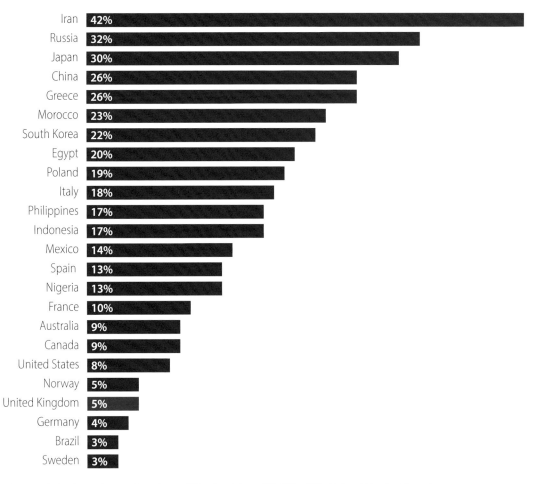

Country	%
Iran	42%
Russia	32%
Japan	30%
China	26%
Greece	26%
Morocco	23%
South Korea	22%
Egypt	20%
Poland	19%
Italy	18%
Philippines	17%
Indonesia	17%
Mexico	14%
Spain	13%
Nigeria	13%
France	10%
Australia	9%
Canada	9%
United States	8%
Norway	5%
United Kingdom	5%
Germany	4%
Brazil	3%
Sweden	3%

Base: 3,056 people aged 18+, surveyed 1 Mar - 9 Sept 2022. Other countries all surveyed in wave 7 of WVS at various points between 2017 and 2022, see WVSA website for sample information of other countries.
Source: King's College London

'Some of the drivers of this extraordinary shift are clear in how we see the contribution of immigrants to our economy and services – we're now the least likely to think immigration increases unemployment, and second from top in thinking that immigrants fill important job vacancies. We're also very likely to say immigration boosts cultural diversity, while very unlikely to think immigration comes with crime and safety risks.

'Politicians often misread public opinion on immigration. In the 2000s, Labour government rhetoric and policy on this issue was more relaxed than public preferences, and arguably they paid the price – but the current government is falling into the reverse trap. Immigration is a classic example of a 'thermostatic' attitude, where policymakers overshoot signals from the public – and then eventually get pulled back. It's time to listen more carefully to public attitudes.'

Technical details

2022 UK data comes from a random probability sample of 3,056 adults aged 18+ interviewed by Ipsos through a mix on face-to-face and online survey methods. Data has been weighted by region, education and age interlocked with gender to be nationally representative.
For analysis of trends over time, data is nationally representative for Great Britain due to a lack of available trend data from Northern Ireland, and is based on surveys of 1,000 or more people aged 18+.
Samples for other countries are all nationally representative and made up of at least 1,000 people. Information on the sampling methodology these nations is available via the World Values Survey Association website.
Data produced for this research is used in wave 7 of the World Values Survey, which included around 90 countries and ran from 2017 to 2022. See the full report for the precise year each country was surveyed. The report focuses

on a cross-section of 24 countries selected based on the availability of reliable and weighted data and then narrowed down, focusing on global coverage (based on the UN's standardised country coding system), regional coverage and population size. This selection gives coverage of 12 of the 17 UN M49 geographic regions across 24 countries, representing almost 50% of the world's population (source: World Bank). Not all questions are asked in each country in every wave of the study, and so the number of countries compared on each question can vary.

23 February 2023

Key Facts

- 68% of the UK public think we should either let anyone come to who wants to or let them come as long as there are jobs available.

- The UK (21%) is least likely to think immigration increases unemployment.

- The UK (70%) is second only to Canada (73%) in believing that immigration strengthens cultural diversity.

- The UK (22%) is least likely to say that immigration causes the crime rate to rise, with countries such as Germany (61%) and Australia (35%) far more likely to hold this view.

www.kcl.ac.uk

How the language of migration put expats on a pedestal – and left immigrants in the dust

Whether it's a conscious or subconscious decision, there's no denying that these terms represent double standards in society's view on who has a right to move freely around the world, writes Nicole Chui.

Growing up in Hong Kong, I was constantly surrounded by people from around the world. From the UK to South Africa and Canada, I was exposed to a number of different cultures in my day-to-day life, especially in school. But it wasn't until middle school, where acquaintances would casually use two distinct terms to define either affluent or poorer areas of the city, that I really began to take notice of the significance of the language of immigration.

Based on what I observed, it was clear that whenever someone referred to a person as an 'expat', they generally tended to be middle to upper-class native English speakers, working in professions such as banking, tech, education or creative roles. When it came to the word 'immigrant', the term tended to apply loosely to both blue-collar workers, and those desperate to flee their birth country in order to make 'a better life' for themselves.

Around a month ago, while FaceTiming a friend who had just moved back to Singapore from London, the extent of those differences became even more pronounced. In the middle of our chat, he mentioned a print magazine called *Expat Living*, and how bizarre it was that among other publications, it was still considered a best-seller in the country despite the dying print media industry. It led me to think about the marketing power of the word 'expat' – clearly a symbol of financial value in society. It placed them on a uniquely aspirational pedestal.

Expats are praised for daring to move to a new country, while immigrants feel pressured to get approval from citizens and assimilate for survival. Whether it's a conscious or subconscious decision, there's no denying that these terms represent the double standards in society's view on immigration. It's not so different here in London, where even after seven years of living here, I'm still confronted by the same forms of hypocrisy, especially in the language the media uses in stories about immigration. Prior to this pandemic, for example, a simple search for the terms 'immigrant' would typically pull up more divisive and sensationalist headlines.

Furthermo...
immigrant
other word

So why

According
associated
and 'poor'.
with expa
Therefore
connotatic

When I ta
an expat
Whereas a
in order to
that this i
much the
it comes t

Often pec
more con
by doing
suggestir
validating

Doe

It is impc
experien
this topi
life living

In popular media, the word 'immigrant' often showcases individual story-lines of struggle, hard work and overcoming hardships. On Instagram, a search for accounts and posts hashtagged with 'immigrant' reveal feeds of documentary-style visuals and text about sacrifice and injustice. Clearly, there's a heavy sense of activism connected to the immigrant experience in the media, in contrast to the image of luxury and privilege that is seen to come with being an expat.

Why? When it comes to the way people treat both groups, the narratives the words we use to describe create an unconscious bias. There's a general feeling that immigrants are associated with negative qualities about their birthplace, whereas expats are commended for living in a country outside of their own. The meanings we've ascribed to these words have a lot to do with connotations about certain races and class systems.

Look at the etymology of the word 'expat' (the short form of 'Expatriate'), for example. It derives from the Latin terms 'ex'(out of) and 'patria' (fatherland). By definition, an expat is just someone who moves to live in a country they weren't born in. Interestingly, the term was most commonly used in the 20th century to describe British servants who were often sent to work abroad against their will. According to Sophie Cranston, a lecturer in human geography at Loughborough University, who spoke to *The Atlantic* about the changing meaning of terms like expat, it was only in the early 90s, that it came to mean what it does now: a descriptor for (typically wealthy) westerners living abroad.

With immigration being brought up more on social and mainstream media, it's also important to note that these terms are being reclaimed. The term 'migrant', which is sometimes used in place of 'immigrant' and often bears the same connotations (although the definitions vary from place to place), seems to have been reclaimed.

In 2015-16, immigration became the hottest political topic in the UK due to the European migrant crisis and Brexit. The Leave campaign heavily focused on villainising immigrants in the media, using anti-migrant propaganda and anti-migrant sentiments to create fear towards them, which subsequently led to their unfortunate victory.

The negativity has since inspired a rise of people from immigrant backgrounds to create movements reclaiming and redefining the meaning of being an immigrant. Groups like Migrants in Culture and Migration Collective are both optimistic examples of how immigrants have used the power of art, statistics, and culture to express different realities and examine issues regarding immigration in the UK.

Migrant Journal, a monthly print and digital magazine with a social media platform that focuses on the experiences of people, goods, and information around the world and the positive impact they have on various spaces, has also embraced the word 'migrant'. The design of their issues are illustrative, with cerebral stories and minimal details that bring a smart and thoughtful impression to 'migrant' labels. They've shown that beyond the stories of people, other things such as objects, spaces and fine art can express the immigrant experience in media in a highbrow manner.

Contrastingly, there's a rise in using social media to poke fun at 'expat' realities and stereotypes. For instance, the popular meme Instagram account @hkmehmeh was founded by a Korean woman who identifies as an expat living in Hong Kong. Her account uses popular internet culture with a mix of Cantonese slang and relatable 'Hong Kong' sayings to create humorous memes that put a light-hearted spin on living in the city from an expat perspective. The account's satirical integration of expatriate stereotypes and local culture makes it entertaining for all people who reside in the city – there's no discrimination with her memes. As a Korean expat, her presence is inadvertently broadening the image of 'expat' and diminishing the assumption that expats can only be white people.

While these labels once showed the double standards of the language of migration, they're beginning to break away from strict definitions. By forging cultural visibility for terms like these, we create opportunities for more open conversations about questioning the need for labels, their effect on our unconscious bias and reclaiming these terms in a positive way.

Platforms that enable positive outlooks on reclaiming negative labels can unite people rather than split them apart. Hopefully, more of this kind of action will allow people to see that regardless of your identity, anyone who immigrates to another country shares more similarities than differences and that labels shouldn't limit or define anyone in what they want to achieve.

17 April 2020

Read

In pairs, look for news articles, in print and online, from the last year about immigration. Read your chosen articles carefully. Select key words/phrases from your articles to demonstrate if the coverage is largely positive or negative.

www.independent.co.uk

Helping refugees when millions more are on the move

Russia's invasion of Ukraine has pushed the global total of refugees to over 100 million. Refugees are like you and me – but not always welcome.

By Helen Womack

'Anyone can become a refugee; refugees are just like you and me.'

The United Nations High Commissioner for Refugees (UNHCR) regularly stresses this message to the public. In six years of writing about refugees, I have come to understand what they go through, how they cope.

This year, Russia's invasion of Ukraine has pushed the global total of forcibly displaced people to a record figure of over 100 million. The exodus of Ukrainian refugees differs from the refugee crisis of 2015, when 1.3 million people from Syria, Iraq, Afghanistan and other countries came over sea and land to reach Europe.

In 2015, many of the asylum seekers were men – either young, single men or married men who did not want to risk the lives of their wives and children on the treacherous sea crossings. They hoped to gain a foothold in Europe so their loved ones could eventually join them.

The refugees coming from Ukraine are overwhelmingly women and children – 90% in fact. They have come alone because their husbands and fathers must stay behind and fight. According to the UN, as of June 22, 7.7 million Ukrainians had fled abroad; as of late May, more than seven million had been internally displaced.

If the profiles of the refugees from 2015 and 2022 differ, so too does the reception they have received. Hungary and Poland built fences to keep out migrants from the Middle East; but these former Communist countries have welcomed refugees from Ukraine with open arms.

It is to some extent understandable that countries welcome refugees from neighbouring states, with similar histories, culture and religion. They think these people are more likely to integrate. But in its annual message for 2022, UNHCR said: 'Every person has the right to seek safety – whoever they are, wherever they come from, whenever they are forced to flee.'

Refugees can be remarkable in their resolve and achievements.

Refugees come from war zones or other situations of extreme danger. They are not on the move from mere whim. Some have been refugees twice over Palestinians who grew up in Syria before war there forced them to flee again, or Sudanese who fled to Libya only to discover that wasn't a safe place either.

During the active phase of flight, when they have to pack up their lives in one or two small suitcases, refugees tend to hold themselves together well. Evidence of trauma, such as survivor's guilt or depression, may come later when they have time to reflect in a safe place.

The refugees I've met have been remarkable in their resolve and achievements. One young Afghan – let's call him M – had only elementary education when he fled the Taliban at age 13. His brother drowned on the sea crossing between Turkey and Greece, and he was left to walk through the Balkans alone. Luckily, he was adopted by an Austrian couple who were both scientists, and now he is doing post-graduate research in medicine in Vienna.

As M said, refugees may see in their young lives what others never see in a lifetime. This experience makes them wise beyond their years and determined to succeed for the sake of those they have lost or left behind.

Refugees come in waves – not waves that threaten to flood us but waves depending on the phase of the war or emergency. In any troubled country, the wealthy leave first, since they often have options abroad. As the situation worsens, more come out, with the poorer leaving later. The elderly and other vulnerable people risk getting stuck.

In Europe, we saw how refugees from Ukraine first came in cars, then by train. At the Ukraine-Slovakia border, I met two oldish sisters from Sievierodonetsk, who had just spent their first pensions on rucksacks. They had nothing to go back to and no idea where they were going. By nightfall they had places in a refugee hostel and were planning to try and find work.

Refugees from Ukraine hope their sojourn will be short.

In response to the Ukraine crisis, the European Union has issued a Temporary Protection Directive, allowing these refugees to stay in member countries, get accommodation and financial support and look for work. Refugees from other countries have had a longer struggle to be accepted.

Refugees – certainly the Ukrainians – initially hope their sojourn will be short and they will soon be going home. But for many, it starts to sink in that their exile is long-term. How quickly they get their lives back on track and integrate into the new society depends on the compassion and efficiency of the host country.

Refugees who are allowed to bring their immediate relatives to join them through family reunification programmes do better than those who are separated from loved ones. And those who manage to learn the language of the new country have a better chance on the labour market. In 2015, Austria and Germany showed the way by providing free language classes for refugees.

In Budapest now, Ukrainian refugees who happen to be teachers have launched pop-up schools, where their kids can pick up the threads of their disrupted education. If they stay, the Ukrainian children will eventually have to go to Hungarian schools, but the Ukrainians may continue to run their classes on Saturdays as a way of keeping their culture alive.

Culture and history are intertwined, and history teaches us that there have always been nomads and settled people.

Some of us are on the move for good reason while others have equally good reasons to stay at home. Interests can clash. In 2022, when one in every 78 people on the planet is a refugee, it is more important than ever that the uprooted and the anchored find mutual understanding.

22 June 2022

Three questions to consider

1. Why does UNHCR say 'anyone can become a refugee'?

2. What problems do refugees face and how do they overcome them?

3. Are you a nomad or someone who has stayed close to home? How can these two groups better understand each other?

Aspen card does not give asylum seekers £175 a week

What was claimed

Every illegal immigrant receives a payment card loaded with £175, which is renewed weekly, in addition to free meals a day.

Our verdict

Payment cards currently worth £40.85 a week are given to eligible asylum seekers who cannot afford food. Those who receive free meals receive much less money.

A post being shared on Facebook includes a screenshot claiming that 'every illegal immigrant' receives a payment card 'pre-loaded with £175.00 (renewed weekly by the Home Office)'. It also claims that this is 'free spending money, on top of their 3 free meals a day'.

These claims are not correct.

It is true that some asylum seekers, some of whom may have entered the UK illegally, receive a payment card from the Home Office.

However, it is not true that every asylum seeker receives one, nor that they receive £175 each week (this is more like the monthly figure), nor that this money is provided in addition to free meals.

How the 'Aspen' card works

People seeking asylum are not able to claim normal benefits and are usually not allowed to work while their case is considered.

The payment card pictured in this Facebook post is known as an Asylum Support Enablement or 'Aspen' card. It is given to asylum seekers who are deemed to be destitute, because they are homeless or do not have money to buy food.

But rather than £175 per week, as the Facebook post claims, the Aspen card currently includes a weekly payment of £40.85 for each person in the household.

Government guidance states that the payment is given to help people buy the things they need, such as 'food, clothing and toiletries'.

The Facebook post also claims this money is given in addition to free meals, but asylum seekers who are housed in accommodation where they receive meals are given an Aspen card with a much smaller amount of money for other essentials. This payment was £8.24 per week in the year from September 2021.

Women who are pregnant or the mothers of young children can receive a further £3-5 per week.

School-age children must attend school, where they may be able to receive free school meals.

Asylum seekers can apply for additional support in exceptional circumstances.

This article is part of our work fact checking potentially false pictures, videos and stories on Facebook. For the purposes of that scheme, we've rated this claim as false because not all asylum seekers receive this money, which currently amounts to £40.85 per week, and is not in addition to food.

Full Fact fights bad information

Bad information ruins lives. It promotes hate, damages people's health, and hurts democracy. You deserve better.

31 January 2023

Further Reading/ Useful Websites

Useful Websites

www.blog.speak.social

www.fullfact.org

www.independent.co.uk

www.inews.co.uk

www.kcl.ac.uk

www.medium.com

www.migrationobservatory.ox.ac.uk

www.news-decoder.com

www.openmigration.org

www.politico.eu

www.refugeecouncil.org.uk

www.telegraph.co.uk

www.theconversation.com

www.theguardian.com

www.weforum.org

page 16: *The Migrants' Paradox* by Suzanne Hall

page 33: **Sources**

Asylum Matters parliamentary briefing, 2018 (PDF)
Asylum statistics 2018: changing arrivals, same concerns
BMA/Refugee Council refugee doctor database, 4 June 2008
Deciding Where to go: Policies, People and Perceptions Shaping Destination Preferences
Home Office Quarterly Immigration Statistics – Year ending June 2022
Reaping the rewards: re-training refugee healthcare professionals for the NHS, October 2009 (PDF)
Report of the Commission of Inquiry on Human Rights in Eritrea, 2015
UNHCR, Global Trends: Forced Displacement in 2020
United Nations 1951 Convention Relating to the Status of Refugees
Women seeking asylum: Safe from violence in the UK?, 2018

Glossary

Assimilation

Assimilation is the process by which immigrants gradually adapt and blend in to the way of life of their host country.

Asylum application

If a person wishes to stay in the UK as a refugee, they must apply for asylum. To be eligible they must have left their country and be unable to go back because they fear persecution. Refugees should apply for asylum as soon as they arrive in the UK.

Asylum seeker

The refugee council defines an asylum seeker as 'a person who has left their country of origin and formally applied for asylum in another country but whose application has not yet been concluded'.

Brexit

An abbreviation that stands for 'British exit'. Referring to the referendum that took place on 23 June 2016 where British citizens voted to exit the European Union. Britain left the EU on 31 January 2020, but a trade deal was finally reached on 24 December 2020.

Economic migrant

Someone who has chosen to move to another country in order to work. Refugees are not economic migrants.

Emigration

Leaving one's native country to live in another state. People emigrate for many reasons, but most often with the aim of seeking out better living and working conditions.

Expat/Expatriate

A person who lives outside their native country.

Hostile environment

A term used to describe policies that aim to make life difficult for migrants to the UK.

Immigrant

A person living in a country to which they are not native.

There are many social and cultural issues associated with immigration, particularly the integration of immigrants into the native population.

Immigration

To immigrate is to move permanently from your home country, and settle somewhere else.

Migrant

A person who is moving or has moved across an international border or within a State away from his/her habitual place of residence.

Migration

To migrate is to move from one's home country and settle in another.

Open border

A border which allows free movement of people or goods between countries with no restrictions.

Refugee

A person who has left their home country and cannot return because they fear that they will be persecuted on the grounds of race, religion, nationality, political affiliation or social group. In the UK a person is officially known as a refugee when they claim asylum and this claim is accepted by the Government.

Refugee camp

A camp that provides shelter/temporary housing for refugees or displaced persons. The world's largest refugee camp is Dadaab in Kenya. The camp hosts 35,000 people in five camps.

Visa

Official permission to enter a country for a temporary stay within a specified time period.

Index